self talk

C O'Brien

BookLeaf Publishing

India | USA | UK

Presentation by *BookLeaf Publishing*

Web: www.bookleafpub.com

E-mail: info@bookleafpub.com

ISBN: 9789357445979

First edition 2022

DEDICATION

To all of us lost adults with young parts doing their best to cope.

ACKNOWLEDGEMENT

My family and friends.
My wonderful partner.

write anyway

this is not what anyone would say is good or
wise
but i write
because a piece of me needs it.
in case one day
someone stumbles across my restless heart
and finds they were not as bad as they thought
and feel less alone

home away from home

i dreamed of my legacy home
the place my cells remember in vivid detail
some stories gifted to me by my mother
stories untold by my father and brothers
of a life i didn't see
a people i never met
blood i do not know
strange to know crystal clear images roil inside
my body that i'll never understand
memories as numerous as the soft grain coral
sand itself
sealed into my skin for me to carry
but not to know or question
who would i be if i had roots there?
who am i now my root system extends across the
sea?

the bleed

i know parts of myself are running rampant
when i start to treat my friends like my family
ignoring calls, avoiding interactions
the guilt associated
the sigh of relief when a connection has been
severed
simultaneous pangs of regret
stagnation, apathy, roiling fear
i didn't dare see it before
wounds left to fester
how do i fight to want to stop the bleed?

T

capital T for trauma is not the issue.
so sheltered, so carefully raised.
equal amounts of love and fear
desperate to protect me
i am grateful in many ways
my mother (& father) filled with fire
it is curious to watch you douse the flames you
spent your whole life stoking instinctively
i carry your capital T trauma and fear inside of
my body
not knowing i was carrying it for you
when it silently screamed out of your pores and
actions
when you could no longer

hidden treasures

5

quietly buried mines are now exploding in my
chest.
tricks and traps placed recklessly and blindly.
unknown.
now the impact.
the fright and fear send some into chaos, some
into battle & my mind into paralysis.
fighting.
crying.
fighting.
breathless.
push with brute force.
unbalanced.
my mind cracks.
i am altered for a moment
but habits die hard.

saplings

the difference between being nice and being
kind is only oceans apart

given tools to obey
given tools to quiet
given tools to comply

as i trip into adulthood
the latest of bloomers in a forest of redwood
trees
searching
searching for curiosity
searching for self acceptance
hoping to make friends of my darkness and
doubt

therapy

"i'm stuck."

"what you're carrying looks heavy."

"i didn't notice i was holding anything."

~ take a breath ~

"are you hurt?"

"something hurts. how do i fix it?"

"we look and ask questions. we'll see what needs fixing afterwards."

"i'm scared."

"we'll go together when you're ready. you'll continue to go together the rest of your life."

true poets

to the true poets who allow the thoughts i cannot
to breach their lips
they feel like they are my own
the ones brave enough to speak truth into
shadowy places
(i am grateful)
the gardeners who transpose deep rooted pain
into abundant fruit & flowers
you allow space to water them with our tears
you physicians who stitch us together at times
with anaesthetic but always from necessity, from
kindness
a reprieve in the battleground
a fire to the apathy
stifled hearts and frightened souls are freer, more
aware
you help us face the days until we can write our
own poetry again

blur

it's so much easier to roll over now
my heart gets harder every day
it's much more comfortable to be walked on
than lift my head up to fight
the tightness in my chest is a tenant rather than
casual acquaintance
relaxing into apathy is a way to live and i live it
everyday
let me hide here.
in my surface opinions, false strength, petty
outrage and pitiable jealousies
breathe out and ignore another day

do the right thing

tell me what to do
i've never learnt to make a decision on my own
just tell me what to do so i can do it right

a close compliment

you are not as eloquent as you think you are
you are not as inept as you think you are

self indulgent

12

my heart hurts with malcontent
my belly is full of everything but satisfaction
my hands are soft from lack of servitude
my feet are cracked by gentle pressures
my back aches from inactivity
my shoulders hunch from starring at my navel
my head is heavy from too much sleep.
i am short today—shorter still tomorrow.
for nothing.

self talk

i loathe having my picture taken
mirrors are stark enemies
compliments make me uncomfortable
but you can be sure i will look myself straight in
the eyes when i tell my heart i hate myself and
my body i am a worthless
watch me comfort and punish myself as i eat
myself to death

competition

i can make myself smaller than you.
so light you won't hear my voice or tread.
i can dodge better, blush more & cram into
cornices like no other.
so silent i forget the vibrations of my voice.
let me echo and mirror all your favourite angles
as i flatten my edges for your pleasure.
my gift to you.

the difference

the difference between being nice and being
kind is only oceans apart

given tools to be nice
given tools to obey
given tools to quiet
given tools to comply

as i trip into adulthood
the latest of bloomers in a forest of redwood
trees
searching
searching for curiosity
searching for self acceptance
hoping to make friends of my darkness and
doubt

permission

who gave you permission?
why do i continue to wait for permission?
why don't i gift myself such permission?

rest

my darling critic, my fierce protector
aren't you terribly tired of holding on so tight?
your barbed words pierce much more deeply
than i would like
perhaps more furiously than you intend
if i take the reigns a while,
would you rest?

grey / gray

how to hold the two
the black and white once served me well but the
grey, the gray is where i find my family
the grey / the gray is where i find my friends
to be filled to the brim with fear and curiosity

illusions

my kind of love is fierce and frightened
she is engulfing and frozen
vital and suffocating
do not seek to be loved by this kind of halting
hiccoughing spluttering love
she's a desolate road of loneliness where when
the whim will take me,
i might dane to give you
a precious moment of time
but retract it as soon as the sprout comes to light
sprinklings of water on parched tongues
she'll evaporate before your eyes, before you
can enjoy it
before you know it
love is consistent
love is right action
in the trenches
the push and pull of explosions and suppression
is not

the body's wisdom

quiet memories in every fibre

stories shouting into the void

i have learnt so well to ignore all of the signs

surgery to separate my head, heart and body

and then i wonder why i am sick

Young friends

Today I played pretend
Like when i was little.

I met myself.

I pretended I was my friend.

I took myself by the hand and asked myself what
I wanted to do today.
I knew I wanted to play outside but I started to
cry first.

As I cried, I sat beside myself and said it was
okay.
I told myself it was okay to feel whatever I was
feeling.
I told myself to let it out.

I waited patiently and told myself you have
nothing to feel sorry about.
I gave myself some tissues.
I told myself not to worry about taking up space
and time.

That's what a friend would do.

A stranger I recognised arrived.
Told me to hurry up, to stop crying.

My friend and I tried to ignore them.

This stranger i recognised tried to talk all over
the conversation my friend and I were having.
Again. Again. Again.

We turned to the stranger this time.
Why?
Why can't we take up space?
Why can't we take up time?
There was confusion..some silence.

I think you need a friend too.

So my friend and I asked some questions of our
own.

When was the last time you were shown
kindness?
Why are you afraid of being seen?
Shadow was tired too.

Come sit with us and join our tea party.
There's no rush today.

We had treats, played outside, drew with chalk
on pavement near home, watched the ducks
swim.

We laughed with each other about how silly it
was that we hadn't seen or played together in
forever.
We cried when we pushed a bit too rough but
said sorry and went out to play some more.

Where were you? we asked each other,
confused.
Playing hide and seek but I didn't think anyone
wanted to find me.

We lay down tired in the bark, breathing heavily
from the running.

Can we be friends again tomorrow?
If I go count this time, will you promise to come
and find me again?